THE ENCHANTED PIG

A Fairy Tale for the Disenchanted

BY

CHARLES LUDLAM

SAMUEL FRENCH, INC.
45 WEST 25TH STREET　　　NEW YORK 10010
7623 SUNSET BOULEVARD　　HOLLYWOOD 90046
LONDON　　　　　　　　　*TORONTO*

Copyright © 1989, by The Estate of Charles Ludlam

ALL RIGHTS RESERVED

CAUTION: Professionals and amateurs are hereby warned that THE ENCHANTED PIG is subject to a royalty. It is fully protected under the copyright laws of the United States of America, the British Commonwealth, including Canada, and all other countries of the Copyright Union. All rights, including professional, amateur, motion pictures, recitation, lecturing, public reading, radio broadcasting, television, and the rights of translation into foreign languages are strictly reserved. In its present form the play is dedicated to the reading public only.

The amateur live stage performance rights to the play are controlled exclusively by Samuel French, Inc., and royalty arrangements and licenses must be secured well in advance of presentation. PLEASE NOTE that amateur royalty fees are set upon application in accordance with your producing circumstances. When applying for a royalty quotation and license please give us the number of performances intended, dates of production, your seating capacity and admission fee. Royalties are payable one week before the opening performance of the play to Samuel French, Inc., at 45 W. 25th Street, New York, NY 10010; or at 7623 Sunset Blvd., Hollywood, CA 90046, or to Samuel French (Canada), Ltd., 80 Richmond Street East, Toronto, Ontario, Canada M5C 1P1.

Royalty of the required amount must be paid whether the play is presented for charity or gain and whether or not admission is charged.

Stock royalty quoted on application to Samuel French, Inc.

For all other rights than those stipulated above, apply to The Estate of Charles Ludlam, c/o Walter Gidaly, 750 Third Avenue, New York, NY 10017.

Particular emphasis is laid on the question of amateur or professional readings, permission and terms for which must be secured in writing from Samuel French, Inc.

Copying from this book in whole or in part is strictly forbidden by law, and the right of performance is not transferable.

Whenever the play is produced the following notice must appear on all programs, printing and advertising for the play: "Produced by special arrangement with Samuel French, Inc."

Due authorship credit must be given on all programs, printing and advertising for the play.

ISBN 0 573 69132 0   Printed in U.S.A.

Anyone presenting the play shall not commit or authorize any act or omission by which the copyright of the play or the right to copyright same may be impaired.

No changes shall be made in the play for the purpose of your production.

The publication of this play does not imply that it is necessarily available for performance by amateurs or professionals. Amateurs and professionals considering a production are strongly advised in their own interests to apply to Samuel French, Inc., for consent before starting rehearsals, advertising, or booking a theatre or hall.

No part of this book may be reproduced, stored in a retrieval system, or transmitted in any form, by any means, including mechanical, electronic, photocopying, recording, videotaping, or otherwise, without the prior written permission of the publisher.

IMPORTANT BILLING AND CREDIT REQUIREMENTS

All producers of THE ENCHANTED PIG *must* give credit to the Author of the Play in all programs distributed in connection with performances of the Play and in all instances in which the title of the Play appears for purposes of advertising, publicizing or otherwise exploiting the Play and/or a production. The name of the Author *must* also appear on a separate line, in which no other name appears, immediately following the title, and *must* appear in size of type not less than fifty percent the size of the title type.

In all acting editions of the Play and in all programs the following credit *must* appear:

"Originally produced by The Ridiculous Theatrical Company in New York City."

COVER BY ROBERT RICHARDS

THE ENCHANTED PIG was first performed in New York City on April 22, 1979 by The Ridiculous Theatrical Company with the following cast and crew:

KING GORGEOUS III ....John D. Brockmeyer
PRINCESS GONDA................... Deborah Petti
PRINCESS WANDA..............Ghislaine Chantel
THE ENFANTA EULALIE IRENE
....Black-Eyed Susan
A PRINCE FROM THE EAST ....Bill Vehr
A PRINCE FROM THE WEST
.... Edward McGowan
A PIG FROM THE NORTH ....Everett Quinton
MOTHER WORMWOOD .... Lola Pashalinski
MOTHER OF THE MOON..........Adam McAdam
MOTHER OF THE SUN...........H.M. Koutoukas
MOTHER OF THE WIND............Julia Pearlstein
BABY..Dexter Dimple

Set Design and Execution: Bobjack Callejo
Costume Design and Building: Gabriel Berry
Lighting Design Lawrence Eichler
Original Music: Peter Golub
Puppet Heads and Masks: Adam McAdam
Dragon Design and Execution: K.K.
Production Stage Manager: Lawrence Eichler
Assistant State Manager: Kevin Kelleher
Light Board: Lauren Feiner, Jeffrey Hartman

CHARACTERS

KING GORGEOUS III
PRINCESS GONDA
PRINCESS WANDA
THE ENFANTA EULALIE IRENE
A PRINCE FROM THE EAST
A PRINCE FROM THE WEST
A PIG FROM THE NORTH, later revealed to be a true prince
A WITCH
THE MOTHER OF THE MOON
THE MOTHER OF THE SUN
THE MOTHER OF THE WIND

ACT I

Scene 1

Fanfare. KING on his throne. The three princesses enter to him.

THE THREE PRINCESSES. You sent for us, Father?

KING. Yes. My dear children, I am obliged to go to the wars. The enemy is approaching us with a large army. It is a great grief to me to leave you all. During my absence take care of yourselves and be good girls; behave well and look after everything in the house. You may walk in the garden, you may sit in the living room, or you may live in the sitting room. But don't go into *that* room. (*Points to a door.*) Into that room you must not enter for harm would befall you.

GONDA. You may keep your mind easy, Father.

WANDA. We have never been disobedient to you.

EULALIE IRENE: Go in peace, Father, and may heaven send you a glorious victory.

KING. Here are the keys to all the rooms of the palace, and don't forget what I told you. Don't go into *that* room.

(*Fanfare. Exit KING. The three princesses twirl and sit, which implies that it is ...*)

Scene 2

Several days later.

GONDA. Sisters, all day long we sew, spin, and read. We have been several days quite alone, and there is no corner of the garden that we have not explored. We have been in all the rooms of our father's palace, and have admired the rich and beautiful furniture. Why should we not go into the room that our father forbade us to enter?

EULALIE IRENE. Sister, I cannot think how you can tempt us to break our father's command. When he told us not to go into *that* room he must have known what he was saying and have had a good reason for saying it.

WANDA. Surely the sky won't fall about our heads if we *do* go in. Dragons and such-like monsters that would devour us will not be hidden in the room. And how will our father ever find out that we have gone in?

(*WANDA and GONDA walk toward the room in slow motion, as if drawn by a magnet. EULALIE IRENE looks on in frozen horror.*)

EULALIE IRENE. No. No. Don't do it sisters. Please don't disobey our father.

(*The eldest takes out the key, unlocks the door, and opens it. An empty room is revealed with a table center with a gorgeous cloth and on it a big open book.*)

GONDA. I wonder what is written in that book. (*Reads.*) "The eldest daughter of King Gorgeous III will marry a prince from the East."

WANDA. (*Reads.*) "The second daughter of King Gorgeous III will marry a prince from the West."

(*WANDA and GONDA laugh and kiss each other.*)

WANDA. Now it's your turn, Eulalie Irene.

GONDA. You read next.

EULALIE IRENE. (*Frightened.*) No no, I don't want to!

GONDA. Come on, don't be a scaredy cat. Read. (*Drags her to the table.*)

EULALIE IRENE. I don't want to read what is written in that book.

WANDA. (*Pushing her face into the book.*) Read!

EULALIE IRENE. (*Turns the page with fear and trembling and reads.*) "The youngest daughter of King Gorgeous III will be married to a pig from the North." (*Faints.*)

WANDA and GONDA. There there. (*Patting her hands and face.*)

EULALIE IRENE. (*Comes to and begins to wail and cry.*) Why did I do it? Why did I read when Father told me not to? (*Sobs.*)

GONDA. How can you believe such nonsense? When did it ever happen that a king's daughter married a pig?

WANDA. What a baby you are! Has not our father enough soldiers to protect you, even if the disgusting creature did come to woo you?

EULALIE IRENE. (*With a heavy heart.*) Yes, I suppose you are right. Oh why, oh why did I disobey Father?

Scene 3

The princesses sit at their spinning wheels.

GONDA. Eulalie Irene, Eulalie Irene. Why don't you sing?

WANDA. Why don't you play?

GONDA. Why don't you gather flowers to put in your hair?

EULALIE IRENE. How can I sing? How can I play? How can I gather flowers to put in my hair? When my thoughts always return to that book in which stood written that great happiness waits for you, my sisters, but that a fate is in store for me such as has never been known in the world.

(*Fanfare.*)

GONDA. Listen! The trumpets. Father has returned from the wars!

(*Enter the KING. There are shouts of joy and merry music.*)

KING. Please, my people, stop for one moment this revelry and merrymaking. And let us pray. (*All fall silent. Kneeling.*) Thank you heaven for this glorious victory I have gained over my enemies who rose against me. Amen.

ALL. Amen!

(The KING rises and the merry music resumes. The three princesses come forward to greet their father.)

KING. Where are my daughters? Where's Wanda and Gonda and Eulalie Irene?

GONDA. Welcome home, Father, how happy I am to see you!

WANDA. Father, Father, how I missed you.

KING. Wanda and Gonda, you look well—and prettier than ever, I might add. But where is Eulalie Irene?

EULALIE IRENE. Here, Father.

KING. And how do you feel? Are you not glad to see me?

EULALIE IRENE. No.

KING. No? What do you mean no? Speak again and tell me yes.

EULALIE IRENE. I cannot lie to you, my father. No, I am not glad to see you.

KING. So young and so untender! And to think I always loved you best. Go to your chamber at once, ungrateful girl, and there remain until you are glad to see me.

EULALIE IRENE. Then there will I remain forever for I cannot lie and say I'm glad to see you. *(She turns to go.)*

KING. Wait Eulalie Irene. You break your father's heart. Tell me child, why have you grown so thin? Why do you look so sad.

EULALIE IRENE. Don't ask me, Father.

WANDA. She's been like this for weeks now.

GONDA. Ever since you went away.

KING. Oh no! I fear the worst. (*Very stern.*) Daughters, come and tell me the truth. Did you do that which I forbade you to do? Did you open that one door I told you not to open?

EULALIE IRENE. (*Bursting into tears.*) Yes! Yes! Forgive me, Father. But that is why I was not glad to see you.

KING. And did you all read from the forbidden book?

WANDA, GONDA and EULALIE IRENE. Yes.

KING. And which one of you led the others into temptation?

(*WANDA and GONDA point at each other guiltily.*)

EULALIE IRENE. It was I, Father. I alone knew better.

KING. (*Wailing loudly and beating his breast with his fists.*) Oh no! Oh no! What have you done? (*The princesses are almost frightened to death.*) Now what has happened has happened and not a thousand words can alter matters by a hair's breadth.

Scene 4

Trumpets sound. Enter PRINCE FROM THE EAST.

PRINCE FROM THE EAST. Hail O King. May your reign be blessed with a plentitude of years! I have come to ask the hand of your eldest daughter.

KING. Her hand? What's wrong with the rest of her?

PRINCE FROM THE EAST. I mean I want to marry her.

KING. Princess Gonda, we have here a prince from the East. He wishes to marry you. What do you say, my daughter?

GONDA. He is a man of goodly parts and as handsome as a prince in a fairy tale. Yes Father, Your Highness, I will gladly marry this prince. I feel I am beginning to love him already.

KING. So be it. And for your dowry take the shadowy forests and champlains rich with plenteous rivers and wide-skirted meads. Of all these parts of my kingdom do I make you lady.

(*Trumpets sound. Enter PRINCE FROM THE WEST.*)

PRINCE FROM THE WEST. Hail O King. May your reign be blessed with health and happiness! I have come to ask the hand of your second daughter.

KING. Princess Wanda, a prince from the West has come to ask your hand. What do you say my daughter? Will you marry him?

WANDA. Yes, Majesty, my Father. For he is comely and straight as a fir tree. I will be his own.

KING. Good. Then for your dowry take another piece of our fair kingdom no less in space, richness, or pleasure than that I gave your sister. Let there be a great marriage feast. Let there be singing, dancing and merrymaking. Eat, everyone, eat! (*Everyone laughs and eats except PRINCESS EULALIE IRENE.*) Eulalie Irene, why do you not sing, or eat, or dance at your sisters wedding?

EULALIE IRENE. Everything has fallen out exactly as it was written in that book. I won't eat. I won't put on fine clothes and dance! I won't! I'd rather die than be made a laughingstock to the world.

KING. There there, my child. You're wrong to be so sad. There is nothing to be sad about.

(*Trumpets blast an oinking sound.*)

EULALIE IRENE. (*Startled and shaking with fear.*) What was that I heard?

KING. It was a trumpet blast.

EULALIE IRENE. No, no dear Father, I think it was the sound of oinking!

(*Enter an enormous PIG FROM THE NORTH.*)

PIG. Hail O King. May your life be as prosperous and bright as sunrise on a clear day!

KING. I am glad to see you well, my friend, but what brings you hither?

PIG. I come a-wooing.

THE ENCHANTED PIG

KING. (*Aside.*) This is amazing. I've never heard so fine a speech from a pig! Something is the matter here. Something *unusual* is definitely the matter here.

PIG. Oink oink. I have come to ask the hand of your youngest daughter.

KING. I would gladly give you anything but that O pig. I'll promise you anything that you wish. But not the hand of my youngest daughter, the Princess Eulalie Irene.

PIG. I won't be satisfied with mere promises. I want the wedding to take place at once.

EULALIE IRENE. Father, protect me, call out your armies, but don't give me in marriage to this pig no matter how fine his speech is.

PIG. Soueee! Soueee!

(*A great oinking is heard outside the palace.*)

KING. What is that sound I hear? (*Goes to his balcony and looks out.*) The castle is surrounded by all the pigs in the world.

PIG. I won't go away until you swear a royal oath that the marriage will take place within a week.

EULALIE IRENE. Don't swear it, Father, don't swear!

(*The great oinking is heard in the streets once more.*)

KING. There is no escape.
PIG. Swear, King, swear.
KING. I swear!

PIG. Good. Let the wedding feast be prepared. But make sure that you prepare it to my specifications. I want the feast to be held in a sty and all the guests to eat from a trough like pigs.

SISTERS and PRINCES. Eeecht!

KING. And what will we serve, O pig?

PIG. Garbage and swill. And after the banquet we'll have dancing and we'll all roll in the mud.

KING. Oh no!

PIG. What did you say?

KING. I said, "just so!"

PIG. And just so it will be. I am going now. But when I return I will expect you to have prepared everything exactly as I ordered it. Farewell for a fortnight O King. (*Exit with a great loud oink.*)

PRINCESS. (*Sobbing and weeping.*) I won't do it! I won't marry a pig. I won't. (*Bursts into tears again.*)

KING. My child, I advise you to submit to fate, for there is nothing else to be done. My armies cannot stand against all the pigs in the world.

PRINCESS. Oh! (*Weeps even more loudly.*)

KING. My child, the words and whole behavior of this pig are quite unlike those of other pigs. I do not myself believe that he always *was* a pig. Depend upon it, some magic or witchcraft has been at work. Obey him and do everything that he wishes, and I feel sure that heaven will shortly send you release.

PRINCESS. (*Choking back her tears.*) If you wish me to do this, dear Father, I will do it.

THE ENCHANTED PIG

Scene 5

The wedding feast. Pigs and people at a trough decked out like a banquet table.

PIGS.
Oink oink oink!
Roll in the mud.
We accept you as one of us.
Oink oink oink!
Roll in the mud.
We accept you as one of us.

PIG. My dearest wife. Why don't you join in the festivities?

EULALIE IRENE. (*Aside.*) This is the most horrible thing I've ever been subjected to. (*Then philosophically.*) But what is a poor girl to do? I suppose I may as well oink and roll in the mud with the rest of my in-laws.

PIGS.
Oink oink oink!
Roll in the mud!
We accept you as one of us.

PIG. I'm waiting, darling.

KING. Remember Daughter, better do as he says until fate sends some solution to your problem.

PIGS.
Oink oink oink!
Roll in the mud!
We accept you as one of us.

EULALIE IRENE.

Oink oink oink!
Roll in the mud! (*She does so.*)

PIGS. Now we accept you as one of us! (*The PIGS all cheer.*)

PIG. Now give me a kiss.

EULALIE IRENE. (*Wipes the PIG's snout with her hankie and kisses it.*) There, my husband.

PIGS. (*Cheer and chant.*)
We accept you.
We accept you.
We accept you as one of us.

PIG. Come my wife, our carriage awaits.

EULALIE IRENE. But where are we going to live? Shall we have a third of your kingdom, Father?

KING. Certainly not. I cannot give my kingdom to the pigs. (*PIGS mutter discontentedly.*) You must go and live in Pigland. Your sisters will divide your share of our domain. (*Tears map in half and gives the pieces to WANDA and GONDA.*)

PIG.
Then come Eulalie Irene
Bid them adieu.
For you will be a queen
In a country new.

(*They get into the carriage and drive off.*)

PIGS.
Oink oink oink!
Roll in the mud!
We accept you as one of us.

THE ENCHANTED PIG

Scene 6

The Pig's dwelling.

PIG. (*Enters carrying EULALIE IRENE across the threshold.*) Here is our new home, my beloved Eulalie Irene. This is where we'll settle down.

EULALIE IRENE. Yes, my lord.

PIG. Don't call me "my lord." I don't like flattery. Call me pig, for that's what I am.

EULALIE IRENE. Yes pig.

PIG. You will live here in my sty and if you wait on me hoof and mouth I promise you that I will never hurt you.

EULALIE IRENE. Yes pig.

PIG. Don't' be afraid.

EULALIE IRENE. I won't be ... afraid.

PIG. You must find my ugliness repulsive.

EULALIE IRENE. I cannot lie, pig.

PIG. I will do all I can to help you forget my ugliness.

EULALIE IRENE. That won't be easy. But thank you all the same, pig.

PIG. But you must promise me something.

EULALIE IRENE. What?

PIG. That you will never look into my eyes.

EULALIE IRENE. Why that?

PIG. Please promise me that.

EULALIE IRENE. No. That will I never promise. To live with someone and never look into his eyes? Why that would make me feel too alone, O pig. I could not bear it.

PIG. Do not defy me, wife.

EULALIE IRENE. Why pig, I think you are more afraid than I. Why do you fear my eyes? Why do you refuse me yours? Let me look. (*She takes the PIG's head in her hands and looks into his eyes although he tries to look away.*) What is it you're afraid I'll see?

PIG. No, please don't.

EULALIE IRENE. (*Amazed at this discovery.*) Why they're kind! They're gentle.

PIG. (*Turning away from her ashamed.*) My heart is kind. But I am a monster.

EULALIE IRENE. I saw great love in your eyes. And sensitivity.

PIG. I'm crude and unrefined.

EULALIE IRENE. Come now. Don't be ashamed. There are many men more crude than you. But they hide it well.

PIG. I know I am repulsive. But Eulalie Irene, if you could ever find it in your heart to love me ...

EULALIE IRENE. Please pig, don't ask the impossible. I can never love you. But I will try to be your friend.

PIG. My heart would break if you ever left me.

EULALIE IRENE. I'll never cause you any pain. I could never be cruel to any animal.

PIG. You called me an animal.

EULALIE IRENE. But you are an animal. You're weeping.

PIG. Forgive me.

EULALIE IRENE. (*Kneeling before him.*) No no, it is you who must forgive me. I was crude.

PIG. It is I who should be kneeling before you.

THE ENCHANTED PIG

EULALIE IRENE. Give me time O pig. Give me time. I will try to love you. I will learn. But not all at once. Please, give me time?

PIG. Thank you Eulalie Irene. (*Yawns an enormous yawn.*) I'm so tired I can hardly keep my eyes open. Good night wife. Good night.

EULALIE IRENE. Why he's fallen fast asleep. Poor thing, he's exhausted. I almost feel sorry for him lying there. Like a big baby pig. He's not really a bad pig ... as pigs go. I'll just tuck him in. (*She pulls the covers up over him and lo and behold the PIG turns into a man.*) Why this pig has changed into a man. Clearly my husband must be bewitched. I think in time I will grow fond of him. Don't hog the covers. (*She lies down beside the PIG and falls asleep.*)

Scene 7

WITCH.
Mumble mumble
Fall and stumble
Elvies tall
And giants humble
Into magic thread
You tumble
There to make the piggie grumble.
Mumble mumble
Fall and stumble
Sigh of mute
Cry of wail
Curly as the piggie's tail

Follow on the piggie's trail
Make the piggie cry and wail
When you tie it on his tail.

    EULALIE IRENE. Who is that I hear singing? It's been so long since I've seen another human being. How good to have someone to talk to for a change! (*Calling out to the WITCH.*) Good Madame! Good Madame! I say good Madame! Over here. Won't you come and talk to me?

    WITCH. What is it you want my dear?

    EULALIE IRENE. It's so good to hear your voice. Why, you're the first human being I've laid eyes on since I left my father's kingdom and came hither to live in the Land of Pigs.

    WITCH. I'm a stranger here myself.

    EULALIE IRENE. What is your name?

    WITCH. The people I help call me Mother Wormwood.

    EULALIE IRENE. Mother Wormwood. But what brings you to Pigland?

    WITCH. I am a woman who knows all the magic arts. I can foretell the future, and I know the healing power of herbs and plants.

    EULALIE IRENE. I shall be grateful to you all my life, old dame, if you will tell me what is the matter with my husband. Why is he a pig by day and a human being by night?

    WITCH. It could be worse. It could be the other way around. I was just going to tell you that one thing, my dear, to show you what a good fortune teller I am. If you like I will give you an herb to break the spell.

THE ENCHANTED PIG

EULALIE IRENE. If you will only give it to me, I will give you anything you choose to ask for, for I cannot bear to see him in this state.

WITCH. Here, then, my dear child, take this thread, but do not let him know about it, for if he did, it would lose its healing power. At night, when he is asleep, you must get up very quietly, and fasten the thread around his left foot as firmly as possible; and you will see in the morning he will not have changed back into a pig, but will still be a man.

EULALIE IRENE. Oh thank you kind woman! How can I ever repay you?

WITCH. I do not want any reward. I shall be sufficiently repaid by knowing that you are happy. It almost breaks my heart to think of all that you have suffered, and I only wish that I had known it sooner, as I should have come to your rescue at once. I must be going now my child, to help others who have need of me.

EULALIE IRENE. Farewell kind woman, and may heaven bless you. (*Exit WITCH. EULALIE IRENE tiptoes to her husband's bed and ties the thread to his foot.*) Ah! The thread snapped!

PIG. (*Awakening with a start and crying out.*) Unhappy woman, what have you done? Three days more and this unholy spell would have fallen from me, and now, who knows how long I may have to go about in this disgusting shape?

EULALIE IRENE. It was a mistake to waken you. We should never wake the man we love. In his sleep he's ours completely. But the moment he opens his eyes, he escapes. Sleep again ...

PIG. Where did you get this thread? Who gave it to you?

EULALIE IRENE. Mother Wormwood.

PIG. Mother Wormwood! *(Thunder, lightning.)* That was the foul witch Sycorax, whose pet dragon I slew. She put this curse on me for revenge. (*Thunder and lightning.*)

EULALIE IRENE. But she seemed so kind!

PIG. I must leave you at once, and we shall not meet again until you have worn out three pairs of iron shoes and blunted a steel staff in your search for me. (*He disappears.*) That is the curse. Farewell.

EULALIE IRENE. (*Begins to weep.*) Wait a minute. These tears and groans will do me no good. I must get up and go wherever fate leads me. But before I do I must go to town and buy me those three pairs of iron shoes and that steel staff. For the sooner a great journey is begun the sooner it is ended. (*Exits.*)

Scene 8

To be depicted with all the resources of the puppet stage. Trees in frightening shapes, weird shadows. The branches tear her hands and hit her face but she presses on. Worn out and overcome with sorrow she arrives at a house.

EULALIE IRENE. At last a house. Perchance whoever lives herein will grant me shelter for the night. (*Knocks at the door. The door opens and a woman's face of silver peeks out.*) Who lives here, pray?

MOTHER OF THE MOON. Who do you think lives here? The Moon.

EULALIE IRENE. Is the moon at home?

MOTHER OF THE MOON. No she's not. I am the Mother of the Moon.

EULALIE IRENE. Oh, let me in I beg of you, that I may rest a little.

MOTHER OF THE MOON. Come in, child, and let me care for you. You look utterly worn out.

EULALIE IRENE. Thank you.

MOTHER OF THE MOON. But tell me child, how was it possible for you, a mortal, to get hither to the house of the moon?

EULALIE IRENE. It's a long story.

MOTHER OF THE MOON. Come inside my child, and tell me your story.

EULALIE IRENE. Thank you, kind goddess. For of a truth I am going to have a baby.

MOTHER OF THE MOON. Come in and let me help you all I can. (*Yells off.*) Hot water and plenty of it. (*They exit into the house and close the door. There is the sound of a baby crying.*)

Scene 9

Enter GONDA followed by PRINCE FROM THE EAST.

PRINCE FROM THE EAST. Did your father spank you for not eating your vegetables?

GONDA. Ay, my husband. By night and day he wrongs me! I am queen now. I am an adult. I won't be treated like a child anymore. I won't!

PRINCE FROM THE EAST. But surely he knows you are a grown woman now and can eat whatever you like?

GONDA. I thought when I got married I would be my own mistress in my own castle.

PRINCE FROM THE EAST. Yesterday he forbade me to go hunting for a week because I kicked his favorite dog.

GONDA. I'll not endure it! He flies off the handle at every trifle. Hourly he finds some fresh excuse to punish us like naughty children.

(*Horns within.*)

PRINCE FROM THE EAST. He's coming, darling. I hear him.

GONDA. I will not speak to him. I'll ignore him and if he speaks to me I'll pretend not to hear.

PRINCE FROM THE EAST. But what explanation will I give?

GONDA. Say I am sick. And if he doesn't like it let him go and live with my sister. She and I have agreed not to let him have his way. He has given the kingdom to us. We are queens. Let us rule him!

PRINCE FROM THE EAST. But Gonda, old fools are babes again and must be kissed and flattered when they feel abused.

GONDA. I won't give in. Remember what I have said. Give him cold looks and freeze him out of the palace. I'll write to my sister Wanda and tell her to do the same (*Exit.*)

(*Enter KING with dog.*)

KING. Ho! What's for dinner? Hello there! Ho! (*To the PRINCE.*) Where's my daughter? Gonda! Gonda! Why doesn't she come when she is called? Gonda! Gonda!

PRINCE FROM THE EAST. So please you, sir ...

KING. Eh? What's that you say? (*Shouting.*) Dinner—ho—dinner! I think the whole world's asleep! Where's my daughter? Did you not hear me, boy?

PRINCE FROM THE EAST. Your daughter is not well.

KING. Well why did you not say so at once, boy?

PRINCE FROM THE EAST. I beg your pardon, sir, but I am king here. And a king's castle is his home.

KING. (*Roaring with laughter.*) King! Oh ho ho! That's a good one! King! You are king because I made you one, pup! And don't forget it.

PRINCE FROM THE EAST. This is a rank offense, sir. How dare you treat me so? I am King.

KING. And who am I?

PRINCE FROM THE EAST. My lady's father.

KING. My lady's father! My horse's tail! You dog! You cur! You mongrel! You poodle!

PRINCE FROM THE EAST. (*Giving him a cold look.*) I beg your pardon! I am none of these, my lord.

KING. Don't bandy icy looks at me! (*Strikes him.*)

PRINCE FROM THE EAST. I'll not be struck, my lord.

KING. Nor tripped neither? (*Trips him.*) You base Babylonian cook! Come on, get up. Here, take my hand. You see how I've helped you up in the world. Now go get my daughter! (*Boots him out.*) King!

(*PRINCE exits. Reenter GONDA with PRINCE hiding behind her.*)

GONDA. Good father, what mad riot is this to kick my husband and call him names? You are a guest in our house. Behave like one, I beg you.
KING. Guest? Guest?
GONDA. Yes, sir, and we are your hosts.
KING. Hosts? And what am I, a parasite? And what am I? And who am I? Does anyone here know me? (*Kneels.*)
GONDA. Please, sir, get up off your knees and don't make a scene. Someone might come along.
KING. Is this King Gorgeous? Does Gorgeous walk like this? Does Gorgeous talk like this? That is: Gorgeously? Are these Gorgeous eyes, Gorgeous cheeks, Gorgeous hair? (*Shouting.*) NO! A shadow of a King am I since I married my sweetest daughter to a pig and went to live with my piggish daughter.
PRINCE FROM THE EAST. Sire, if you can't say anything nice about someone then you shouldn't say anything at all.
KING. Then I'll say nothing. I have yet another daughter left. I'll go to her. When she hears of the way you treated me she'll scratch your eyes out.
GONDA. Please try to understand my side of it, Father.
KING. Father? I see no fathers here.

THE ENCHANTED PIG

GONDA. I mean you, Father.
KING. The father of a sow? That's a boar. Please, don't let me bore you. (*Exit.*)
GONDA. I fear what he may do.
PRINCE FROM THE EAST. You may fear too far.
GONDA. Better than trust too far. (*They exit.*)

Scene 10

Enter MOTHER OF THE MOON and EULALIE IRENE with the baby in her arms.

EULALIE IRENE. I shall always be grateful to heaven for leading me hither, and grateful to you that you took pity on me and on my baby, and did not leave us to die. Now I beg one last favor of you. Can your daughter, the Moon, tell me where my husband is?
MOTHER OF THE MOON. She cannot tell you that, my child. But if you will travel towards the East until you reach the dwelling of the Sun, he may be able to tell you something. Here is a roast chicken to eat. And be very careful not to lose any of the bones because they might be of great use to you later on.
EULALIE IRENE. Thank you Mother of the Moon, for your hospitality and good advice. I'll throw away this pair of iron shoes for I have worn them out. And I'll put on the second pair. I've got my baby and my chicken bones and I'll be on my way. Adieu.
MOTHER OF THE MOON. Farewell, brave woman. The East is that way. (*Points the way.*) May my

daughter light your way by night. As the sun lights it up by day.

Scene 11

Journey through the Mountains.
EULALIE IRENE crawls, she falls, she jumps from peak to peak. The flints tear her feet and elbows. At length wearied almost to death she reaches the palace of the Sun.

EULALIE IRENE. This little piggie went to market ... (*Knocks at the door. The door opens and out peers a golden face.*) Are you the Mother of the Sun?

MOTHER OF THE SUN. I am, but I am astonished to see a mortal from the distant earthly shores at my doorstep. What a piteous sight you are with all you have suffered. What brings you here, mortal woman?

EULALIE IRENE. I have come to ask your son if he knows where my husband is.

MOTHER OF THE SUN. I will ask him for you. But you must hide in the cellar so that he doesn't notice you on his return home, for he is always in a bad temper when he comes in at night.

EULALIE IRENE. But how in the world is it possible for the sun to be angry? He is so beautiful and so good to mortals.

MOTHER OF THE SUN. This is how it happens; in the morning when he stands at the gates of paradise he is happy, and smiles on the whole world, but during the day he gets cross, because he sees the evil deeds of men, and that is why his heat becomes so scorching; but in the evening he is both sad and angry, for he stands at the gates of death; that is his usual course. From there he comes back here. But come inside and let me give you a roast chicken to eat. And be careful to save all the bones. (*Exit.*)

Scene 12

KING. Ah, here at last after weary journey come I to the home of my better daughter. *(Enter WANDA and her PRINCE as king.)* Good morrow to you both.

WANDA. I am glad to see Your Highness.

KING. Wanda, I think you are. If you were not ... if you were not I'd not believe you were my daughter ... I'd doubt your mother's fidelity. Ah, beloved Wanda, your sister is a snake.

WANDA. Good Father, my sister is no snake!

KING. I am mistaken. A vulture then!

WANDA. Nor no vulture neither.

KING. She's something hideous.

WANDA. Father! How can you speak of my sister so? Why, she's beautiful.

KING. She treated me like a piece of furniture!

WANDA. I cannot think my sister in the least would fail her obligation to you.

KING. My curses on her!

WANDA. O sire, you are old. Confer your cares on younger strengths and let yourself be ruled and led. Go back to my sister and tell her you are sorry.

KING. Ask her forgiveness? After what she did to me? (*Kneeling.*) Dear daughter, I confess that I am old; age is unnecessary: on my knees I beg that you'll give me clothing, bed and food.

PRINCE FROM THE WEST. (*Aside to Wanda.*) This is appalling.

WANDA. Good sir, no more; these are unsightly tricks: return you to my sister.

KING. (*Rising.*) Never, Wanda! She and her husband gave me cold looks. She struck me with her tongue, most serpent-like upon the very heart. May all the stored up vengeances of heaven fall upon her ungrateful head. Strike her young bones, you damp and poisonous airs, with lameness.

PRINCE FROM THE WEST. Fie, sir, fie!

KING. You nimble lightnings dart your blinding flames into her scornful eyes! Infect her beauty! May her skin shrivel and all her hair fall out!

WANDA. O the blest gods! So will you wish on me when the rash mood is on!

KING. No, Wanda, you I will never curse.

(*Trumpet.*)

PRINCE FROM THE WEST. What trumpet's that?

WANDA. I know it. It's my sister's. She sent me a letter saying she would be here soon.

(*Enter GONDA and PRINCE FROM THE EAST. GONDA and WANDA kiss and join hands.*)

KING. O Wanda, you would kiss her and take her by the hand?

GONDA. Why should she not, my lord? What have I done wrong?

PRINCE FROM THE EAST. It's better not to argue with him.

PRINCE FROM THE WEST. You're right. The man's insane and will only curse us more at every word we speak.

WANDA. In this my sister and I are of one mind. If you live with us you live under our law.

KING. I gave you all—

GONDA. You took your time in giving it!

WANDA. Your second childhood's coming on. Let us be your parents now.

KING. Parent abusers! I'll give you both the spankings of your lives! Come girl, over my knee! (*Seizes GONDA.*)

GONDA. Help! Husband! Sister! Help!

(*KING attempts to spank GONDA.*)

WANDA. Oh no you don't! It's our turn now. Come princes, help me turn the tables. Let's spank the king as hard as we are able!

(*They free GONDA and the two princesses take the KING over their knees and spank him.*)

KING. Ah, how sharper than a serpent's tooth it is to have a thankless child!

(*They release him.*)

PRINCE FROM THE EAST. That really did my heart good.

PRINCE FROM THE WEST. He had it coming to him.

WANDA. Sir, I hope you've learned your lesson. And behave yourself from now on.

GONDA. From now on you'll obey the rules of my house.

KING. No.

GONDA. Yes.

KING. No, I say.

GONDA. I say, yea.

KING. No no, I will not!

GONDA. Yes yes, you will!

KING. By Jupiter, I swear no!

GONDA. By Juno, I swear yes!

KING. I will not do it. I would not do it. I could not do it. Detested hags, I'll bother you no more. I'd sooner live in a tree like an ape or in a sty like a pig than live with you brats! Away! Away! (*Exits.*)

PRINCE FROM THE EAST. I'm worried that the king has no place to stay tonight.

(*Distant thunder.*)

PRINCE FROM THE WEST. Come inside, there's a storm brewing.

WANDA. A night in the forest with the hoot owls will teach him a lesson.

GONDA. Yes, let the forest be his school.

PRINCE FROM THE EAST. But come inside. It's a wild night. (*They all exit.*)

Scene 13

The palace of the Sun.
The door reopens.

EULALIE IRENE. What did your son say when you asked him where my husband is?

MOTHER OF THE SUN. He said he knew nothing about him and that your only hope is to inquire of the Wind.

EULALIE IRENE. Then there's nothing to be done but pack up my chicken bones and baby, put on the third pair of shoes, for the second pair is all worn out, and with my staff in hand set out on my way to the Wind.

MOTHER OF THE SUN. Good-bye courageous woman, and may my son shine on you, but not too harshly.

EULALIE IRENE. Good-bye. Good-bye.

Scene 14

Journey through fire and ice. After which EULALIE
  IRENE arrives at an enormous cave in the side of
  a mountain where the Wind lives.

EULALIE IRENE. (*Knocking at a gate before the mouth of the cave.*) Mother of the Wind! (*Knocks again.*) Mother of the Wind. Please answer!

MOTHER OF THE WIND. But how did you, a mortal woman, find your way here beyond the world's portals to the dwelling of the Wind?

EULALIE IRENE. I came upon one mountain of flints after another out of which tongues of fire would flame up. I passed through woods which had never been trodden by human foot, and had to pass fields of ice and avalanches of snow. I nearly died of these hardships but I kept a brave heart and finally came to this place.

MOTHER OF THE WIND. And here will you rest. I'll see to that, brave woman.

EULALIE IRENE. But could you tell me, Mother of the Wind, where I might find my husband?

MOTHER OF THE WIND. My son, the Wind, has spoken of him often. It seems he has been living in a thick woods, so thick that no axe has been able to cut a way through it; there, shunning humankind, he's been living in a shoe, because he's so unhappy, he doesn't know what to do.

EULALIE IRENE. Thank you, thank you. I knew I'd find him one day!

MOTHER OF THE WIND. Here, eat this chicken and save the bones. Go by the Milky Way which lies across the sky at night and wander on till you reach your goal.

EULALIE IRENE. (*With tears in her eyes.*) Thank you, Mother of the Wind. (*Exits.*)

Scene 15

Enter all three MOTHERS.

MOTHER OF THE MOON. Well met by starlight, sisters dear.

MOTHER OF THE SUN. How long before the rooster crows?

MOTHER OF THE WIND. The night wears on and little dreamers wrapped in slumber sleep.

MOTHER OF THE MOON. All our children sleep?

MOTHER OF THE SUN. One-half of the world sleeps while the other works and plays.

MOTHER OF THE MOON. And who are our children? I forgot.

MOTHER OF THE WIND. All those who need a mother mother we.

MOTHER OF THE SUN. We must make haste in what we have to do. The dawn tiptoes creeping up behind would take us by surprise. You called me here to help our children, did you not, Mother of the Wind?

MOTHER OF THE WIND. I did.

MOTHER OF THE SUN. Last night I heard you wail for Eulalie Irene. I never go to earth. I hate it there. The stories that my son recounts would make you shun it too if once you heard them.

MOTHER OF THE WIND. The wind would tell a tale too if he could. And he can.

MOTHER OF THE MOON. But he whispers it.

MOTHER OF THE WIND. Sometimes he howls. Eulalie Irene is married to a pig.

MOTHER OF THE SUN. All loves are tested in the fire of suffering.

MOTHER OF THE MOON. How can we help?

MOTHER OF THE WIND. There's a bad mother who does not believe in love.

MOTHER OF THE MOON. For every three good mothers there's one bad.

MOTHER OF THE SUN. Nay, not so many! Not one in four under the sun.

MOTHER OF THE MOON. This one's bad, I say. Unloved herself she won't let others love.

MOTHER OF THE WIND. Then we must find her love. Send her love. Bend her love. Bind her love.

MOTHER OF THE MOON. But hark, the dawn is breaking! Listen (*They all bend to listen. A crash of breaking glass is heard.*) The stars are fading.

MOTHER OF THE SUN. The sun, my son, is rising.

MOTHER OF THE WIND. Farewell, my sisters. Sisters, farewell. And pledge we. Pledge we. Not to fail. By wind ...

MOTHER OF THE SUN. By sun ...

MOTHER OF THE MOON. By moon ...

MOTHER OF THE WIND. For living mothers and for mothers lost ...

ALL THREE MOTHERS. We'll bring together loves no matter what the cost. Farewell.

Scene 16

The journey through the Milky Way and through the dense forest.

EULALIE IRENE. I have endured hardships greater than any human woman. I have worn out my third pair of iron shoes in my wanderings and my iron staff has become quite blunted. Have I wasted my time? Perhaps I should just give up. But what is this here in this thicket? Why it is just the sort of house the

THE ENCHANTED PIG

Mother of the Wind described. It has no windows. (*Walks all the way around the house.*) And no doors. What am I to do? How am I to get in? The only door is on the roof. The chicken bones! I've dragged them all this weary way. Surely the mothers would not have told me to take such good care of them if they had not had some good reason for doing so. Perhaps now, in my hour of need, they may be of use to me. (*She takes the bones out of the bundle and thinks for a moment.*) Perhaps if I just place the two ends together. Why they stuck! Why it seems that if I put all the bones together they will make a ladder. (*She does this and they do. As soon as one step is finished, she stands upon it and makes the next one, and then the next until she comes close to the door.*) But what's this? The last step ... I haven't got enough bones to make the last step! I must have lost one of the bones! What will I do? Without the last step the whole ladder is useless. I have it! (*Takes out a knife.*) I'll cut off my little finger. (*Does so.*) And make the last step of the ladder. It stuck! *[(Alternate business: if the ladder isn't possible or dismemberment objectionable, use bones as keys in the lock of the front door.)*

EULALIE IRENE. But what is this here in this thicket? Why, it's just the sort of shoe the Mother of the Wind described. The door's locked. How will I get in? The chicken bones! I've dragged them all this weary way. Surely the Mothers would not have told me to take such good care of them if they had not had some good reason for doing so. Perhaps one of the bones will fit this lock. I've heard of skeleton keys.

THE ENCHANTED PIG

(*She tries bones. The last one opens lock.*) It fits! (*She enters shoe.*) Home at last!]

EULALIE IRENE. (*Entering the house.*) Why, everything here is in perfect order. Come my baby. We'll take a little food and here we'll rest. This little piggy went to market (*Giggles.*), this little baby stayed home.(*Awwww*), this little baby had ...

BABY. Zucchini.

EULALIE IRENE. Why zucchini?

BABY. Meatless Wednesdays.

EULALIE IRENE. And this little baby had none. (*Oh no!*) And this little baby cried ...

BABY. Wee, wee, wee, wee, wee.

EULALIE IRENE. All the way home.

BABY. Hope he made it in time. Snort, snort, snort...

EULALIE IRENE. Stop that. (*She takes out baby bottle.*)

PIG. (*Entering.*) What's this? A ladder of bones with a finger at the top? Some fresh magic must be at work here! I'm getting away from here. (*BABY laughs.*) Perhaps there is a witch inside my house. I won't climb that ladder. It may be a trap. I know ... I'll turn myself into a dove. Then no witchcraft can have power over me. (*Thunder. Turns into a dove.*)

[*Or:*

PIG. (*Entering.*) What's this? My door is unlocked. And there's a pile of old chicken bones. Some fresh magic must be at work here. I'm gettin' out of here. (*BABY laughs.*) Perhaps there is a witch inside my house. It may be a trap. I know ... I'll turn myself into a dove. Then no witchcraft can have power over me. (*Thunder. Turns into a dove.*)]

THE ENCHANTED PIG

(The dove flies into the house and lands next to EULALIE IRENE.)

EULALIE IRENE. Ah little dove! Do you know where my husband is?
DOVE. Coo coo.
EULALIE IRENE. How I've suffered for him!
DOVE. Coo.
EULALIE IRENE. I've worn out three pairs of iron shoes and blunted a steel staff in my quest through water, fire, stones, and ice. Not to mention the fact that I've had nothing to eat but chicken the whole way.
DOVE. Coo coo.
EULALIE IRENE. I would do anything to change my husband from a pig into a man.
DOVE. Coo coo coo!!!

(Enter WITCH.)

WITCH. Coo on my little dove! Coo! Coo! Coo! If it's a dove you want to be, remain a dove. Be always a dove!
DOVE. Coo coo!! Coo! Coo!
EULALIE IRENE. (*Startled by the WITCH's sudden appearance.*) Agh! Nasty lady! Nasty, nasty lady! You are the cause of all my troubles. You're the author of my sad travail! You, you are to blame. Yes, you!
WITCH. Fie, I say, fie! What are these vain recriminations to one who's scorched by hell's

hyperequatorial climate into a lean mark, hardly fit to fling a rhyme at?

    EULALIE IRENE. Return my husband from that piggy-shape, O hag, and I will do for you whatever you wish. Please!

    WITCH.
Then by strange art will I knead fire and snow
Together, tempering the repugnant mass.
With liquid love all things together grow
Through which the harmony of love can pass;
And fairer shape out of my hands will flow—
A living image, which will far surpass
A handsome prince in a looking glass.
A sexless thing 'twill be, and in its growth
It will develop no defect of either sex
Yet all the grace of both.
So let her be a tree and he a dove
And they remain together in their love.

(EULALIE IRENE turns into a tree.)

    EULALIE IRENE. A tree? A dove?
    DOVE. Coo coo!
    WITCH.
From her matted roots to her gnarled heart,
He'll fly about her and nest in her hair.
So they might live and never be apart,
He'll coo to her, to him her leaves will whisper there.
On this very spot with matted roots she'll grow,
Her true identity none but he shall know!
    EULALIE IRENE.
A tree? A dove? (*To the dove.*)
Then you are he?

THE ENCHANTED PIG

You are my own true love?

DOVE. Coo.

WITCH. And now that I have done what you asked, my pretty, give me your first born child!

VOICE OF KING. *(Off.)*

O Fright! Not fright but truth in hoot owl shapes.
O Crimes! Not crimes but custom's careless kids.
O Mad! Not mad but muddled modern man.

WITCH. Agh! Someone's coming. I'll hide. *(Hides behind tree.)*

KING. *(Enters raving.)* O fright! O crimes! O mad as mad can be. I must sit down and rest me underneath this tree. *(Sighs.)*

WITCH. Be false, my heart, I must dissemble here. 'Tis he! 'Tis he! I thank thee heaven that thou hast heard my prayer and sent me King Gorgeous. Now be strong. Be strong my heart! I must dissemble here. *(Aloud.)* False friend or true?

KING. A true friend to the true; fear not, come hither. So, you can tell fortunes?

WITCH. Not in the dark. Come nearer to the fire. Give me your hand. It is not crossed I see.

KING. *(Putting a piece of gold in her hand.)* There is the cross.

WITCH. Is it silver?

KING. No 'tis gold.

WITCH. There's a lady who loves you. And for yourself alone.

KING. Fie! The old story! Tell me a better fortune for my money, not this old woman's tale!

WITCH. You are passionate, and this same passionate humor in your blood has marred your fortune. Yes, I see it now—the line of life is crossed by many marks. Shame! Shame! Oh you have wronged the maids who loved you! How could you do it?

KING. The maids you speak of are my daughters. But they never loved me.

WITCH. How do you know that?

KING. A little bird in the air whispered the secret.

DOVE. Coo coo. Coo coo. Not true. Not true.

WITCH. There, take back your gold! Your hand is cold like a deceiver's hand! There is no blessing in its charity! Your daughters needed a mother. Where is she now?

KING. Each of my daughters had a different mother. But they all died in childbirth.

WITCH. The curse. The curse. The curse of unrequited love! Long ago you loved a maid, a maid you met at a ball. But you lost her love. Lost her almost forever. Your daughters need a mother. Find her again, your first love, and mend your fortunes mending hers, and take her as your lover.

KING. How like an angel's speaks the tongue of woman, when pleading in another's cause: her own! That is a pretty little shoe upon your foot. Pray give it me.

WITCH. No; from my foot shall that never be taken!

KING. Why, 'tis but a shoe. I'll give it back to you, or if I keep it, will give you gold to buy you twenty such.

WITCH. Why would you have this shoe?

KING. A traveler's fancy, a whim and nothing more. I would fain keep it as a memento of the Gypsy camp at Guadalajara and the fortune teller who told me

THE ENCHANTED PIG 45

to wed a maid I loved long ago and lost ... Pray let me have the shoe.

WITCH. No, never! Never! I will not part with it even if I die. For there is only one other like it in the whole world and I lost that. Lost it with my love.

KING. Your love? What, dead?

WITCH. Yes, dead to me. And worse than dead. He is estranged! And yet I keep this slipper. I will rise with it from my grave hereafter to prove to him that I was never false.

KING. (*Aside.*) Be still my swelling heart! One moment still! (*To the WITCH.*) Come, 'tis the folly of a lovesick girl. Come, give it to me or I will say it is mine and that you stole it.

WITCH. Oh, you would not dare to utter such a falsehood! Besides it would be your word against mine! What proof have you?

KING. Perfect proof, for I have the other. (*Shows the other glass slipper.*)

WITCH. 'Tis thou! 'Tis thou! Yes yes, my heart's elected! My dearest dear Victorian! My soul's heaven! Where hast thou been so long? It's me. It's me: Cinderella.

KING. Why didst thou leave me, my dearest Cinderella?

WITCH. At midnight my coach was to turn into a pumpkin, my gown to rags ... I was so embarrassed. But why didn't you come to look for me?

KING. The kingdom is so vast, there were so many maidens, how could I have found you?

WITCH. You could have tried the glass slipper on every maid until you found the one it fit.

KING. I never thought of that! Here, put it on now and let's forget we ever parted. (*Puts the slipper on her foot.*)

WITCH. Had you not come ...

KING. Don't reprimand me.

WITCH. I would have gone on and on doing evil, so bitter was my heart.

KING. Forgive me, sweet, for what I made thee suffer.

WITCH. I've done a terrible thing. I turned Eulalie Irene into a tree and her prince I imprisoned in a dove.

KING. Undo the spell, I pray.

WITCH. Alas, I cannot. For when love came back into my heart the powers of black magic left. I am no longer a witch, just a woman in love.

KING. Then, Cinderella, you die! For the deeds you did when you were still a witch, you shall be burned alive!

EULALIE IRENE. No no. Mercy, Father! Have mercy on her. Mercy mercy. (*She ceases to be a tree but becomes a woman once more and falls on her knees before her father. The dove becomes a pig.*)

WITCH. Mercy! Who spoke that sacred word? Who pleads for me?

EULALIE IRENE. I did, Mother.

WITCH. O God, she calls me Mother. What power has turned you into a human being once again?

EULALIE IRENE. The power of love.

WITCH. You called me Mother.

EULALIE IRENE. I called you Mother once before but there was wormwood in it.

WITCH. Forgive me, Eulalie Irene?

EULALIE IRENE. I forgive you. But my husband is still a pig.

WITCH. Blessed be the power of love, for it can work miracles. It can call back the dead from death's dark realm. Love was denied me and curdled the milk of human kindness in my breast. But you, you can do it.

EULALIE IRENE. (*Humbly.*) What can I do?

WITCH. You can love. You can forgive. And so, mighty child, you can do everything. I cannot use my powers, but you can. Go to your love. Lay your hand upon his heart and call his name. Then with the help of god your love will hear your voice and feel your love and he will turn into a man.

EULALIE IRENE. (*Goes to the PIG. Lays her hand upon his heart.*) But how can I speak his name? I don't know it. I've never known it! I've always called him Pig. What is your name, Pig? Tell me your name.

PIG. That you must guess. For it is forbidden that any pig should tell his name. Unless you can guess my name I will never turn into a man.

EULALIE IRENE. Is it Rumplestiltskin?

PIG. No, it's not.

EULALIE IRENE. Is it Aloysius?

PIG. No.

EULALIE IRENE. Is it Jake?

PIG. No.

EULALIE IRENE. Is it Tom, Dick or Harry?

PIG. No no no!

EULALIE IRENE. Is it Heathcliffe?

PIG. No.

EULALIE IRENE. Is it Fred?

PIG. No.

EULALIE IRENE. Is it Matthew, Mark, Luke or John?
PIG. No no no no.
EULALIE IRENE. Is it Willie?
PIG. No.
EULALIE IRENE. Is it Charles?
PIG. No.
EULALIE IRENE. Is it Adam?
PIG. No.
EULALIE IRENE. Is it Anthony?
PIG. No.
EULALIE IRENE. Is it Bart, is it Brad, is it Burke?
PIG. No it's not no it's not no it's not no it's not!
EULALIE IRENE. Is it Zeke?
PIG. Nope.
EULALIE IRENE. Then I know it. I will whisper it in your ear. If I'm wrong, tell me and I will go on guessing forever. Because you must be somebody and sooner or later I'll guess who. (*She whispers in his ear.*)
PIG. That's right! (*He turns into a handsome prince.*)
EULALIE IRENE. Why, you are a prince.
PRINCE. Yes, but my ancestors did not believe in fairy tales and so the fairies put this curse on our house.

(*Suddenly there is a great commotion heard off. WANDA and GONDA enter from opposite directions each pursued by a gentleman pig.*)

WANDA. (*Screams.*) Get away from me you disgusting beast!

GONDA. (*Screams.*) Don't touch me! Don't touch me!

PIGS. Oink oink oink!

KING. What is the matter? What's wrong?

WANDA. My husband's turned into a pig!

GONDA. Mine too!

WANDA. I want a divorce!

GONDA. Yes yes, a divorce as quickly as possible.

PRINCE. You should ask Eulalie Irene's advice. For she had that very same problem and solved it. (*Laughs, embraces EULALIE IRENE and kisses her, then he goes out with the others.*)

(*The WITCH lags behind for a moment and calls to EULALIE IRENE.*)

WITCH. My child, pardon my inquisitiveness, but what *was* the pig's name after all? I mean the prince's name.

EULALIE IRENE. Why, couldn't you guess? I'm surprised at you of all people! It was Charming. Prince Charming.

WITCH. Of course. (*They exit. Together.*)

THE END

COSTUME PLOT

PRINCESS WANDA: Blue dress with farthingale

PRINCESS GONDA: Green dress with farthingale

PRINCESS EULALIE IRENE: Yellow and white dress with farthingale. LATER: She becomes disheveled and is turned into a tree

KING GORGEOUS III: Orchid color doublet; Pumpkin pants and hose; Gray hair and beard; Gold crown

WITCH: Black and gold gown; Black conical hat with veil

PRINCE FROM THE NORTH: Helmet trimmed with orange fur; Orange and turquoise coat and pants trimmed with fur

PRINCE FROM THE SOUTH: Blue doublet, pants, and hose; Blue cape

THE PIG: Pig mask; Gray jacket with tails, and black pants. It is a fat suit in one piece -- it must break away very quickly to later reveal the Prince in a red doublet, red and white striped pumpkin pants, a red capelet, and black Prince Valiant wig

PIGS AT WEDDING: Elaborate wedding costumes

MOTHER OF THE MOON: Sparkling white and silver

MOTHER OF THE SUN: Sparkling gold

MOTHER OF THE WIND: Sparkling blue and gray

THE ENCHANTED PIG

PROP LIST

Keys, Embroidery hoop, Wedding veil & flowers, Party favors, House shaped like shoe, 3 pairs of iron shoes, a baby, Chicken bones, Dove puppet, Pair of glass slippers, Large map which the King tears to divide the kingdom, Spinning wheel, Small book, Veil for other princesses and pigs, Food for feast, Piece of thread, Steel staff, 3 roast chickens, Knife, Gold coin, Table with a huge book on it.

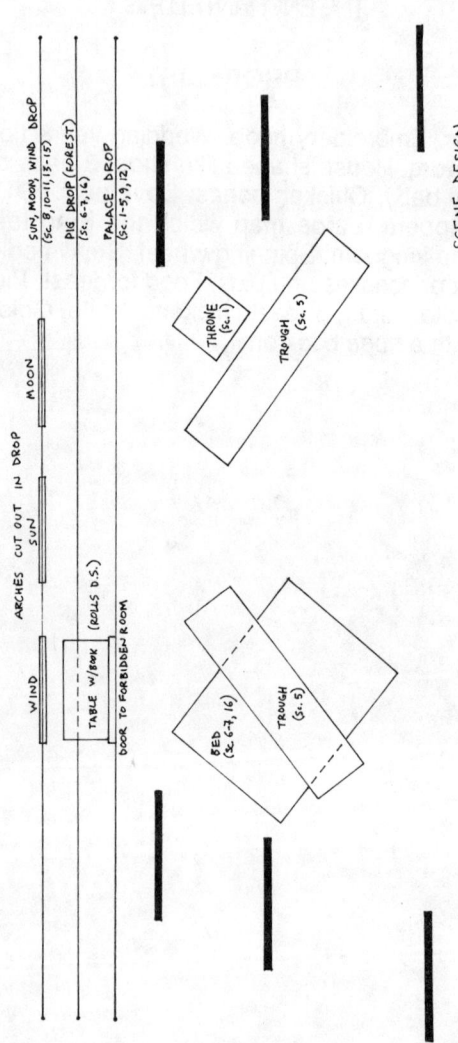